IMAGES
of America

NAZARETH

FIRST HOUSE. The First House in Nazareth was built by the Moravians in 1740 as lodging while they constructed the large stone building known today as the Whitefield House. The log structure later became home to the Single Sisters in the Moravian community. The house was razed in 1864, but a stone marker denotes the site where the building stood. (Courtesy of the Moravian Historical Society.)

ON THE COVER: NAZARETH INN. The Nazareth Inn was the first hotel in New Nazareth, the area of Center and Main Streets laid out in 1771. The inn was built by the Single Brothers of Christian's Spring, opening for business in 1772. It was situated on the road from Bethlehem where, much later, stagecoaches would pass on their way to Belvidere, New Jersey, or Mauch Chunk, Pennsylvania (present-day Jim Thorpe). The cross streets near the inn now bear the names of these two popular destinations for people traveling through the town. (Courtesy of the Moravian Historical Society.)

IMAGES
of America

NAZARETH

Susan F. Ellis with
the Moravian Historical Society

ARCADIA
PUBLISHING

Published by Arcadia Publishing
Charleston, South Carolina

Printed in the United States of America

Library of Congress Control Number: 2019951197

For all general information, please contact Arcadia Publishing:
Telephone 843-853-2070
Fax 843-853-0044
E-mail sales@arcadiapublishing.com
For customer service and orders:
Toll-Free 1-888-313-2665

Visit us on the Internet at www.arcadiapublishing.com

This book is dedicated to the first Moravian settlers who arrived on May 31, 1740, spending their first nights under a large oak tree on the Ephrata Tract, and to all the people since then who proudly call Nazareth home.

CONTENTS

ACKNOWLEDGMENTS

Much gratitude and appreciation are due to the staff and volunteers of the Moravian Historical Society (MHS) who helped bring this book to life. The expertise of former MHS operations manager, Christopher Malone, was invaluable as he spearheaded the initial organization and content of the book. Gerald Kroboth picked up where Christopher left off and diligently scanned and organized hundreds of historical images from the Moravian Historical Society's photographic collection. I am truly grateful to MHS volunteer Barbara Dietterich for her assistance with writing the captions and for her knowledge of the Moravians and of Nazareth. Many thanks are given to Dr. Scott Paul Gordon, chair of the Moravian Historical Society publications committee, for his expert guidance, historical fact-checking, and proofing assistance. Many other community members also provided assistance by filling in the gaps of the Moravian Historical Society's collection. Dick Boak, retired archivist for the C.F. Martin & Co, assisted with securing the Martin Guitar images and with obtaining the images of the Andretti family. Other organizations that contributed photographs include the Jacobsburg Historical Society, Lehigh Cement, the Memorial Library of Nazareth and Vicinity, the Nazareth Greater Valley YMCA, Kraemer Yarns, Holy Family Parish, and St. John's Lutheran Church.

All images in this book, unless otherwise noted, are from the collection of the Moravian Historical Society.

INTRODUCTION

In Nazareth, Pennsylvania, Moravians made their first permanent settlement in America. Moravians originated in Europe and trace their history back to 1457 when followers of Jan Hus (1369–1415) formed the Unity of the Brethren (or Unitas Fratrum in Latin). The most famous minister of the Unity of the Brethren was Bishop Jan Amos Comenius (1592–1670), who became known as "the Father of Modern Education." By the time of his death, however, the Unity had been driven underground.

Comenius had hoped for a rebirth of the Unitas Fratrum, and in the 1720s, that dream appeared to come true. In 1722, Count Nikolaus Ludwig von Zinzendorf (1700–1760) allowed a group of Protestant refugees from Moravia to establish a village on his estate, which they named Herrnhut. Because of the place of origin of the first settlers of Herrnhut, the Herrnhuters became known as the Moravians.

In 1735, a group of Moravians headed to Savannah, Georgia, to serve as missionaries to American Indians and other area settlers. Unfortunately, they faced insurmountable difficulties. By 1740, many were disheartened and returned to Europe. Nine took passage to Philadelphia. The English evangelist George Whitefield had proposed that the Moravians construct a "school and orphanage for negro children" on his recently purchased 5,000-acre property, called Nazareth. This decision marked the beginning of Moravian activity in this part of Pennsylvania.

Progress on the stone building was slow because it was a very rainy summer, and by the fall of 1740 it was clear that the building would not be completed in time for winter. Eleven Moravians set to work on a log building, now called the Gray Cottage. The Moravian workers, led by their pastor Peter Boehler, had already hurriedly constructed one log house next to the stone building, in which they lived for the summer (it was razed in 1864; a stone now marks the spot of this First House). They completed the foundation for the massive building now called the Whitefield House in the summer and fall of 1740, but work stopped when Whitefield objected to their theology and ordered them off his property.

In need of a new home, the Moravians turned to a wealthy Pennsylvania merchant named William Allen. On April 2, 1741, Allen sold the Moravians 500 acres of land at the junction of the Monocacy Creek and the Lehigh River, where they began a new settlement. Count Zinzendorf visited the fledgling settlement in December 1741 and named the community Bethlehem. During this visit, the Moravians also purchased the Nazareth tract from Whitefield. The Moravians returned to Nazareth, and work on the Whitefield House was completed in 1743. This is the spot where Nazareth began. From here, the community developed several nearby farms, designed to produce raw materials for the industries and trades, which were developed by the Moravians in the nearby settlement of Bethlehem.

Unlike most Protestant churches, which were national or ethnic churches, the Moravians had members from many different countries and cultures. Members of several different Native American tribes, especially Delaware, Mohican, and Iroquois, also joined the church. The Moravians who came to this area of Pennsylvania from Europe were primarily German, but as many as 20 different languages were used in church services. No other organization in America was so multilingual and multicultural.

One of the most distinctive features of the 18th-century Moravian Church communities of Nazareth and Bethlehem was that members were organized in groups called "choirs," according to their age, sex, and marital status. These communities typically had the following choirs: Children, Boys, Girls, Older Boys, Older Girls, Single Brothers (18 and older), Single Sisters, Married Couples, Widowers, and Widows. Each choir had a leader, and regular church services were held for each choir. Some choirs lived in their own choir houses. A choir house would typically have a common dormitory in the attic, a Saal (chapel) on the second floor, living quarters, a dining hall, and workshops. In Moravian choir houses, aristocrats and commoners lived, slept, ate, and worked together without regard for rank. Bethlehem and Nazareth were perhaps the most egalitarian communities in the Western world at this time. The choirs gradually lost their importance during the 19th century. While regular church services for the choirs ended in the 19th century, annual choir festivals continued for many years. The Schoeneck Moravian Church in Nazareth continues to celebrate the choir festivals today.

In 1742, as Bethlehem and Nazareth were becoming organized, it was decided that everyone would work for the common good without receiving any pay. In return, the community would provide food, lodging, and clothing. This was called the General Economy. This system enabled Moravians to send out people as preachers and missionaries, while others worked the lands, produced goods, and taught the children. The General Economy consisted of Bethlehem, Nazareth, Christian's Spring, and Gnadenthal. In 1756, a total of 1,132 people were part of the Economy. Because of these large numbers, the economy became difficult to manage, and it was terminated in 1762.

Initially, Nazareth was specifically Moravian by charter, and only those of the Moravian faith could own property. In 1856, the town opened to non-Moravians who were then allowed to live and work in the town. Downtown Nazareth, as we know it today with its Center Square, was laid out in 1771. Even though Nazareth was exclusively Moravian, it was not an isolated community. Situated at the crossroads of major transportation routes, Nazareth was an active, multicultural center for trade and industry.

As Nazareth opened to non-Moravians, it also grew. Industries including textiles, cement production, and agriculture attracted immigrant populations, and the town's diversity expanded from a predominantly German origin to include Italians, Polish, Austrians, and Czechoslovakians.

The textile industry in Nazareth flourished with two successful companies: the Nazareth Waist Company and the Kraemer Hosiery Company. By the turn of the 19th century, the Waist Company employed 450 workers who produced 2,500 dozen garments per day in 400 different styles. In 1887, Henry Kraemer and Hans Jacob Nolde left the Nazareth Waist Company to begin the Kraemer Hosiery Company with 31 employees. In 1889, new machinery was acquired, and the number of employees almost doubled, with production increasing two and one-half times. By 1894, the company grew to 285 employees, and the building was enlarged, more machinery was added, and a new patent for a singeing machine was received in 1897.

Perhaps the biggest change to Nazareth came with the discovery of cement in the late 19th century and the production of the high quality "Portland" cement. The cement boom brought an influx of immigrants, and the borough's population doubled and added a rich variety of ethnic diversity.

During the 20th century, many of these early industries continued to thrive, including the world-renowned C.F. Martin Guitar Company, which has been family-owned and operated since 1833. By mid-century, at least three large cement companies surrounded the Nazareth borough area and employed hundreds of laborers. Nazareth was also home to the Nazareth Speedway, a one-mile tri-oval paved track of Indy and USAC (US Auto Club) racing fame, and is home to racing champions Mario Andretti, Michael Andretti, and third-generation driver Marco Andretti.

Today, Nazareth is a sprawling community surrounded by suburbs. However, visitors can still trace Nazareth's 18th-century beginnings. Much of the Borough of Nazareth is listed on the National Register of Historic Places with more than 500 structures, both residences and commercial buildings, erected between 1740 and 1938.

One

THE BARONY OF THE ROSE

Nazareth is often referred to as the "Barony of the Rose," which relates to older English legal customs regarding land ownership and to the status of Pennsylvania as a proprietary colony. When, in 1731, Laetitia Aubrey (1678–1745), daughter of William Penn, took possession of the 5,000-acre tract later known as the Nazareth Tract, it was established as a "manor." The holder of a manor was allowed to hold a court baron. In return, the holder of the manor supplied the lord with labor, with produce, or with a payment of cash. In this case, Aubrey agreed to pay "one red rose" on June 24 of each year to the proprietors of the colony.

When Whitefield discovered that his finances would not allow him to proceed with his Nazareth plan, Moravian leaders in England negotiated to buy the entire barony. On July 16, 1741, it officially became Moravian property.

The Nazareth tract was acquired by Pennsylvania through the 1737 Walking Purchase, which expelled the Lenapes who occupied the land. One Lenape group, however, led by Captain John, continued to occupy this area. By 1742, pressure from Pennsylvania and compensation from the Moravian leader Count Zinzendorf compelled Captain John to move a few miles north. He occasionally visited the Moravians at Nazareth until his death in 1747.

Upon recommendation by Henry Antes, Nazareth was separated into five communities called the Upper Places, including Nazareth; Gnadenthal ("Gracedale," Dale of Grace), a settlement farm established in 1745; Christian's Spring, organized between 1747 and 1749, where young men and boys were apprenticed to master craftsmen; Friedensthal (Vale of Peace), a Moravian settlement from 1749 to 1767 with an important mill; and the Rose Inn ("the Rose"), established in 1752 for visitors to the settlements.

Christian's Spring became an important training site for many trades: boys learned to be shoemakers, weavers, scribes, and rifle makers. The site also had a dairy, a distillery, and a brewery, which provided the beer for Bethlehem's Sun Inn. In 1771, the communal economy was disbanded, and in 1796 Moravian authorities ended the economy of craftsmen and apprentices and instead established farming families.

Nazareth remained a restricted congregational community for Moravians from 1740 until 1856, when those outside of the Moravian faith were allowed to own property and live and work in the town.

THE GRAY COTTAGE. Completed in approximately one month, the log structure known as the Gray Cottage was finished in 1740 and, along with the First House, became the primary living quarters for the Moravians before the Whitefield House was completed in 1743. The Gray Cottage has served many purposes, becoming the first Moravian school for boys in 1743 and later serving as a home for widows, a lodging for retired missionaries, and then a private dwelling. Now in the possession of the Moravian Historical Society, it stands as the oldest surviving Moravian structure in North America.

THE WHITEFIELD HOUSE. Construction on the Whitefield House began in 1740, but the building known as the "stone house," and later, the Ephrata House, was not completed until 1743. The building housed the first town settlers and was a communal residence for married couples, the first place of worship in Nazareth, the communal nursery for Moravian children, and the Moravian school for girls. It served as a haven for non-Moravian refugees during the French and Indian War and later became an early home for the Moravian Theological Seminary. Until the early 1990s, it was apartments for retired ministers and missionaries on furlough.

PETER BOEHLER. Peter Boehler, a German Moravian bishop and missionary, was sent to the Americas in the early 18th century to spread Moravian piety among Native Americans and white settlers in Georgia and other American colonies. In 1740, he migrated with other Moravians to Pennsylvania, to help found the towns of Nazareth and Bethlehem. Pastor Boehler led the small group of Moravians who constructed the First House, the Whitefield House, and the Gray Cottage.

THE WHITEFIELD HOUSE WITH 1906 ADDITION. The stone house was designed with a combination of Germanic and Georgian architecture. The third story served as a dormitory, the upper attic for storage, and the first and second floors as common, worship, and workshop spaces. The basement served as a kitchen and dining hall. In 1906, noted local architect A.W. Leh extended the building to the east by 30 feet to provide additional space, electricity, plumbing, and heat. The last tenants moved out of the apartments in 1990, allowing the entire structure to be used for the museum and headquarters of the Moravian Historical Society. The building is listed on the National Register of Historic Places.

DER RUHEBERG. The first burial ground within the settlement of Nazareth, the Ruheberg, meaning "hill of rest," was positioned on the highest point within the village, convenient as a central position for all the Upper Places. The graveyard was in use between 1744 and 1762 and was the resting place of 67 Christians. The first burial in the graveyard was in 1744 for George Kremser. Although commonly referred to as "the Indian Cemetery," that name is a misnomer, as only four Native Americans were buried there: two women and two children. This photograph was taken on May 9, 1918, during the dedication of the observation tower on the graveyard. The Bethlehem trombone choir played from the second story of the tower to a large assembly of people.

GOD'S ACRE. Moravians refer to their burial yards as "God's Acres." The site for a more convenient graveyard, closer to the settlement, was established in 1756 by Moravian bishop Augustus Gottlieb Spangenberg. Gravestones in Moravian cemeteries are white and flat, symbolizing equality in death. Each Moravian was buried not with family members but within their choir based on gender, marital status, and age; there are sections for Boys, Girls, Single Brothers, Single Sisters, Married Men, and Married Women.

GOD'S ACRE GATE. The gate shown was the entrance to the 1756 and present Moravian Church Cemetery. The inscription on the east side of the gate in German translates to "[Because] I live, you will also live." On the west side in English was written, "The body rests in hope."

THE NAZARETH PLANTATION WITH WAYNE COTTAGE. Six farms on the barony lands were planned, and families suitable to farm them were sent from Europe to settle them. These farms became known as the Upper Places. South of the Whitefield House tract, orchards, gardens, and fields were tended to feed and supply the 33 couples, known as the Second Sea Congregation, who arrived in 1744. In May 1745, eight families moved into a newly built Familienhaus to settle the first planned farm, known as Nazareth Plantation. The Wayne Cottage on South Whitfield Street was used as a bakery and then home to village mechanics. Positioned at an angle to present-day Whitfield Street, the cottage may have quartered colonial soldiers in 1756 led by Capt. Isaac Wayne, father of Revolutionary War soldier "Mad Anthony Wayne."

THE ROSE INN. The Rose Inn opened in 1752 as a guest house for travelers who were visiting the town or passing through. The completed building contained seven rooms, a kitchen and a cellar, with a stable and springhouse added later. Two of its most famous guests were Richard and John Penn, sons of Pennsylvania proprietor William Penn. In 1755, during the French and Indian War, settlers from the north fled to Nazareth seeking protection. Palisades were built around the Rose Inn, the Whitefield House tract, and other Moravian settlements. In November 1755, nearly 60 refugees sheltered at the Rose, which also quartered many soldiers. Officers slept indoors and troops outside. The Moravians sold the Rose Inn in 1771, and in 1858 it was torn down. Today, a stone marker denotes the site where the inn stood.

CHRISTIAN'S SPRING. Established on a 1,500-acre parcel of land in 1747 with a combined gristmill and sawmill, the settlement was named for Count Zinzendorf's son, Christian Renatus, the spiritual leader of single men in the Moravian church worldwide. The community was designed to be a living and working community for Single Brothers and the boys they trained in various trades.

CHRISTIAN'S SPRING TRADES. Groups of Moravian boys were sent to Christian's Spring to learn trades. Boys learned to be shoemakers, weavers, scribes, as well as rifle makers. Native Americans often stopped by to have their guns repaired, so, in 1763, a gun-stocking shop was built, with Andreas Albrecht as the master. The site included a dairy, a distillery, and a brewery, which provided beer for Bethlehem's Sun Inn. The settlement was very active and saw the brothers producing, among other things, bricks, honey, tobacco, and hay. The communal economy there was disbanded in 1771, and the economy of craftsmen and apprentices was eliminated in 1796. The shoemaker's shop is pictured above.

CHRISTIAN'S SPRING BUILDING. The stone building pictured here is the only structure from 18th-century Christian's Spring that survives today.

18

GNANDENTHAL. Gnadenthal means Dale of Grace in German. Located about one and one-half miles west of Nazareth, Gnadenthal was begun with six families occupying a large house on December 2, 1745. The area was founded as a large plantation for married families who farmed to support the agricultural needs of the General Economy for both Nazareth and Bethlehem. In 1837, the Northampton County Commissioners purchased the 365-acre farm for the Alms House, commonly known as the County Poor House. By 1940, the site consisted of about 20 buildings—12 of which were farm buildings. Farmland provided vegetables, livestock, and poultry to feed the residents. Now occupied by the Gracedale Nursing Home, today it is part of the county's Department of Human Services, providing long-term care and rehabilitative services to residents.

THE FRIEDENSTHAL GRISTMILL. A fourth farming community, located about two miles northeast of Old Nazareth, Friedensthal (meaning Vale of Peace) was chosen because of its proximity to the Bushkill Creek. This Upper Place contained a gristmill, powered by the creek, which was completed and in production in 1750. As pictured above, the gristmill later burned, with only stone walls standing.

BARN AT FRIEDENSTHAL. Along with farming, Friedensthal was also the site of the region's first printing press operated by John Brandmueller, who came from a long line of printers in Basel, Switzerland. He had arrived in 1742 as part of the First Sea Congregation of 58 passengers from Germany, sent to settle the area.

THE VILLAGE OF SCHOENECK. The village of Schoeneck was built on the proposed Moravian village of Gnadenstadt as a "society," a less strict community of Moravians. The new settlement received its name, which means "beautiful corner" in German, in June 1762. The Schoeneck Church celebrated its first communion service in October 1762. The village also had a school with 28 pupils and laid out its own God's Acre (cemetery) just north of the church on what is now Beil Avenue. Schoeneck's second church, designed by William Henry II of Nazareth and completed in 1793, is depicted here. In 1826, a stone parsonage was added to the north side of the church, forming one complete stone building.

INTERIOR OF 1793 SCHOENECK CHURCH. This 1887 photograph shows the interior worship space of Schoeneck's 1793 church.

CENTER SQUARE AND NEW NAZARETH. The intersection of Center and Main Streets, known as "the Circle" or "Center Square," was the location where surveyor Georg Golkowsky laid out the area known as New Nazareth in 1771. Here, Moravians could build private homes and businesses on church-owned land.

CENTER SQUARE CANNON. The Parrott Rifle Cannon, an army surplus from the Civil War, is located inside the Circle on the square. The cannon was added in 1906 to honor the war veterans of Nazareth. The black globes atop the concrete pillars at the entrances to the Circle are actually old bowling balls from the Holy Family Club in town. Looking closely, one can see the finger holes in some of them.

CHRIST HOUSE. On the southeast corner of the Circle, the first building dating from 1771 was a stone structure, the home and hat manufactory of Jacob Christ. This was the first industry in New Nazareth. Many visitors to the town for several generations came to buy his famous "stove pipe" beaver skin hats. The stone structure is now covered in stucco and was reconfigured in 1890 with Victorian turrets and gingerbread trim.

FIRST STORE. The first Moravian community store was built in 1772 near the Jacob Christ home. The store was operated by the Village Committee of the Moravian Church. Originally of stone, it is now stuccoed and houses the law offices of Peters, Moritz, Peischl, Zulick, and Landes.

THE GOOD INTEND. The town's first fire engine was called the "Good Intend." In 1791, an open structure called the Market Building was erected in the circle. It housed a market, the town's first fire engine, the Good Intend, and a water tank. Vendors set up stalls in and around the structure on designated days. Like many of the buildings in Nazareth, the Market Building was razed in 1857.

THE CARRIAGE WORKS. The Carriage Works, begun by John C. Leibfried in 1848, occupied space on the east side of the Circle. The carriage and blacksmith shop were owned by the Leibfried family until 1874, when it was sold to John H. Kreidler and Owen Michael. In 1905, the building was sold to Max J. Ziegler and Morris D. Frable, who moved the business, then known as the Nazareth Vehicle Works, to Progress Avenue.

FIRST PRIVATE DWELLING. On June 28, 1771, Peter Worbass from Bethlehem chose a plot of land on the south side of West Center Street, behind the present 1861 Moravian Church. By September, he had erected a dwelling, and on December 16, he moved into the first private dwelling in Nazareth.

SECOND STORE. Just south of the present-day post-office, the second community store for Nazareth was designed in 1796 by William Henry II, son of famed patriot William Henry of Lancaster. William Henry II was trained as a joiner as well as a gunsmith, and he designed both the 1793 Schoeneck Church and Bethlehem's first bridge in 1794. The store was run by Christian David Senseman in 1798. The building housed a shop on the first floor and family dwellings on the second.

Horse-Drawn Sleigh. An early photograph of the Circle shows the present Nazareth Moravian

Church in the center of the image with the second community store to the right.

View of
The Single Brethren's House
at Nazareth Penn?. as originaly built r,
before any alterations were made.

№ 1   Warden's Room (Pfleger)
  2   Tailor Shop front. Brethrens Room in the rear.
  3   Shoemaker Shop.
  4   Weaving Room.
  5   Sleep Hall
  6   Attic
  7   Prayer Hall.
the Basement contained the Kitchen & Dining Room
Size of Building 55 feet front 27 feet deep.

Explanation

drawn and presented
to the
Moravian Historical Society
October 1863
by
Rufus A Grider.

Sketched Oct. 1863 by
Rufus A Grider.

SINGLE BRETHREN'S HOUSE. The Single Brethren's House was where the unmarried men of Nazareth lived and where some practiced their trades. Built in 1773, the stone building had sleeping quarters and workrooms as well as a Saal (chapel). Later, it was one of the town's first shoe and boot stores, operated by Frank Kunkel. It became Star Janitor Supply Company, selling paint, tools, and hardware. Almost unrecognizable today, Mycalyn Florals now occupies part of the building. South of the Single Brethren's House on Main Street was the home of William Henry II, who operated a gun shop there in 1781. He test-fired his long rifles in the alleyway next to the workshop, upsetting his neighbors and earning reprimands from the church elders.

BLACK ROCK SPRINGS. Black Rock is a wooded area of Nazareth owned by the Moravian Church west of the Nazareth Borough Park. It is a serene, quiet place providing walking paths, a spring, and at one time, a springhouse. The cool and peaceful forested area was a favorite retreat for early residents who picnicked at the springhouse. It is reported that in 1804, a druggist from Philadelphia was paying $50 per ton for the black mineral paint found in large quantities at Black Rock. The overseers' committee of the church considered erecting a plaster of Paris grinding mill for the paint, creating a new source of income for the congregation. The operation of the mill began in May 1817.

COUNT NIKOLAUS LUDWIG VON ZINZENDORF. Zinzendorf, a Lutheran nobleman, led the mission movement of the Unitas Fratrum (the renewed Moravian Church) and helped establish the settlements of Nazareth and Bethlehem. Thinking Zinzendorf would make his permanent home in Nazareth, the Moravians erected the Manor House for the count, with the cornerstone laid on May 3, 1755, and dedicated in 1756. Zinzendorf never returned to America, however, and he died in Saxony in 1760.

THE MANOR HOUSE. The Manor House was the largest building in colonial America built for a single family. The building's first floor was used as the second Saal (German for chapel) of the Moravian congregation until the 1840 Church was built. Rooms in the Manor House were used by both instrument builder David Tannenberg and artist John Valentine Haidt.

Two

Early America's Preeminent School for Boys

Nazareth Hall can trace its beginnings to 1743, when a school was started in the Gray Cottage for Moravian boys. The school moved a number of times before returning to Nazareth to the Manor House in 1759. By 1785, the school became a tuition-based school open to sons of non-Moravians as well. Later, it attained wide fame as a "classical academy."

Over its 180 years in operation, closing only for a brief period of six years due to economic hardship, Nazareth Hall was at the forefront of progressive education in America. In 1785, the Reverend Charles G. Reichel, who served as principal of the school for 17 years, implemented a revised curriculum. The school emphasized classical education as well as vocational training and religious instruction. Nazareth Hall was one of the first institutions of learning to teach subjects such as geography. Bookkeeping, surveying, and industrial drawing were taught in the 1850s.

In 1862, principal Rev. Edward H. Reichel organized his pupils into a uniformed cadet company and introduced military drill. With the Civil War being fought, the climate of the school changed from Moravian pacifism to the discipline involved in military training, and the school came to be known as Nazareth Hall Military Academy. Certainly, the military training was beneficial to graduates of the hall during the Civil War. Five cadets became generals in the Union army, and three graduates became Confederate army generals. Of the 262 former students fighting in the Civil War, 234 fought for the North and 28 for the South. Ninety Union men became commissioned officers.

In 1840, the first freestanding Moravian church structure was begun. Later, the white building was added next to the church. This building, known as the "First Rooms," was where the older boys lived. On the far end is the building erected in 1819, known as the President's House, where the school's headmaster lived. The former 1840 Church became the gymnasium for the boys' school with Nazareth's first indoor swimming pool on the first floor and basement.

As the second decade of the 20th century came to a close, so too did the school. Nazareth Hall's glorious existence came to an end when Nazareth Hall Military Academy closed in 1929, after 186 years of scholastic achievement.

The Nazareth Hall Tract was added to the National Register of Historic Places in 1980.

NAZARETH HALL. The area of Nazareth Hall, now known as Hall Square, began in 1755 with the erection of the Manor House for Count Zinzendorf. In 1759, a boarding school for Moravian boys moved into the house. On October 3, 1785, the school was reorganized as the "Paedagogium," or boarding school, a tuition-based school for boys from age 7 through 12, now accepting non-Moravians. In 1787, the first non-Moravian student, Joseph Shaw, son of a Philadelphia Quaker merchant, entered the school. With an esteemed headmaster and faculty such as famed musician and composer David Moritz Michael, the school welcomed students from all over the country and from foreign places such as St. Croix and Jamaica. Visitors to Nazareth Hall were frequent, and in 1841 the famous Cherokee Indian chief John Ross toured the school. Ross then sent his sons to Nazareth Hall.

NAZARETH HALL MILITARY ACADEMY CADETS. Discipline to accompany lessons came as Nazareth Hall evolved into a military academy after 1862. The boys were divided into room companies, which became the social and residential units. Assignments to companies were by age; class divisions were based on academic proficiency. At most, there were five companies with 10–20 cadets per unit. In February 1894, the students and faculty petitioned the administrative board to wear uniforms during the school day, except for "play period." At first, parents could make uniforms at home with patterns supplied by the school. Outdated uniforms were also donated by the armed forces for cadets to wear.

MILITARY DRILLING. In the center of the complex of buildings at Nazareth Hall was a grassy area, which became the parade grounds for the cadets.

The Cenotaph and 1840 Church. Unveiled on June 11, 1868, a 35-foot stone cenotaph bears the names of the Union dead who had attended Nazareth Hall. The cost of the war memorial, constructed by William Struthers of Philadelphia, was $3,000 and was financed by the alumni. In all, 27 Union boys and five Southern boys died in the Civil War.

Class Photograph. The cenotaph became a favorite spot for class pictures, as seen in this photograph from 1881.

THE 1840 CHURCH. The 1840 Church became the third house of worship and the first freestanding church for the Moravian congregation. After 22 years, the congregation outgrew the building, and a larger church was built in the Circle in 1861. The sanctuary of the 1840 Church then became a lecture hall for the boys' school and later the gymnasium.

PRINCIPAL'S HOUSE. Also known also as "the Headmaster's House," the brick English Federalist building was constructed between 1817–1822. Later, a Victorian section was added to the south along with porches and dormers. Attached later to the right rear of the house were a locker room and shower room for the boys. In 1941, the Will R. Beitel's Children's Home, Inc., moved into the former Headmaster's House, providing housing and care for orphaned children. In September 1966, the last child vacated the home, which is now owned by the Moravian Church.

THE GYMNASIUM. In the 1860s, the former 1840 Church became the gymnasium for the cadets at Nazareth Hall Military Academy. The basement was dug out in 1905 and included an indoor swimming pool in the lower level, fed by a local spring. Thought to be one of the first indoor pools in the country, it is said that the boys learned to swim quickly since the water was so cold, rarely reaching 60-plus degrees.

THE FIRST ROOMS. This 1923 photograph shows the library at Nazareth Hall, located between the 1840 Church and the President's House. The First Rooms would have also included the classrooms.

GEOMETRY CLASSROOM, 1916. The school offered subjects including reading, writing, and arithmetic; the English, German, Latin, French, and Greek languages; and history, geography, mathematics, music, and drawing. A five-to-six-hour period of instruction was held daily, except for Sunday, with a two-hour-and-fifteen-minute noon intermission used as a study period. Beginning in the 1850s, more subjects were added, including bookkeeping, dictation, surveying, industrial drawing, and chemistry. Until 1802, English was spoken three days per week with three days of German. On Sunday, both languages were spoken. For eight German words spoken on an English day, and vice versa, a fine of one cent was imposed.

WOODSHOP, C. 1920. Nazareth Hall offered vocational training, as did most schools of that time. Industrial drawing, printing, photography, typewriting, telegraphy, and stenography were also offered.

HALL BOYS. Even though the boys were under supervision by faculty at all times, they found moments of leisure.

SINGLE SISTERS' HOUSE. The stone building to the right facing the Manor House is the Moravian Single Sisters' House, built in 1784 for the unmarried women of the congregation. The Sisters lived in the house adjoining the school buildings of the Hall to help care for the boys. Here, they served as cooks, laundresses, seamstresses, and more for the boys.

DINING HALL. At one time, the boys' dining hall was in the Single Sisters' House. The food there was said to be plain and wholesome. Food was grown on the farm since there were several large tracts of land on the school property. In 1785, a "pay school" for girls was begun there, lasting only a brief time. In 1807, a theological seminary was begun in the basement of the building, remaining there until 1813.

THE PLEASURE GARDENS. On August 28, 1786, a small park was laid out to the west of the Hall buildings. In later years, the area became known as the Pleasure Gardens. It was a series of landscaped terraces, planted with specimens brought from around the world by Moravian missionaries and having a brook fed by a spring at the bottom. Bridges crossed the stream, a pavilion was added, and rare varieties of trees and shrubs grew there. Sketches of the gardens show a pond and a structure for reflection. With its long sloping hill from the Moravian cemetery at the top to the Headmaster's House at the foot of the hill, the Hall boys enjoyed sledding there, as have generations of Nazareth residents.

A MAYPOLE. Accounts of Nazareth Hall include reports of festive events attended by local Nazareth residents. One such celebration was the traditional May Day and Maypole dance of cadets and female partners. Ticketed plays and musical productions were also presented and attended by families and residents.

FLAG CEREMONY. This photograph depicts cadets firing the cannon and lowering the flag in 1924. The cadets enjoyed the local parades in Nazareth and Bethlehem, and townspeople came to the Hall in the evening to watch the flag being ceremoniously lowered. Encampments on the grounds and on the field across Center Street following examinations were a sight enjoyed by residents and visitors. Cadets marching from the Hall to church services at the 1861 Moravian Church on the Circle was a spectacle every Sunday.

SPORTS AT NAZARETH HALL. Besides military drills and marching, athletic events were popular at the Hall, which stressed physical fitness in its advertising. Tennis was offered, but football became the most popular competitive team activity. Teams from the older boys at Nazareth Hall competed against public schools such as Nazareth High School. They practiced on the field across Center Street from the parade ground.

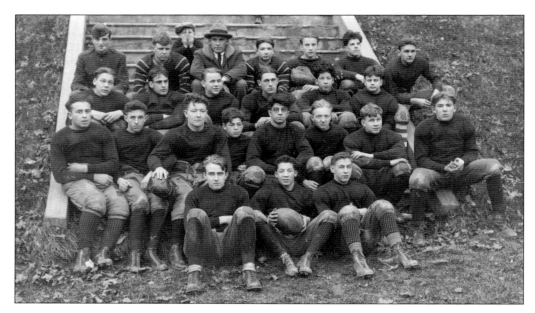

NAZARETH HALL FOOTBALL. The Nazareth Hall football team of 1925 poses with its coach. The *Hall Boys*, a monthy magazine from 1914 to 1918, indicates that Nazareth Hall competed against teams including Nazareth High School, Moravian College, Stroudsburg High School, Allentown High School, and Easton High Reserves. Pictured below is the Nazareth Hall football team of 1922.

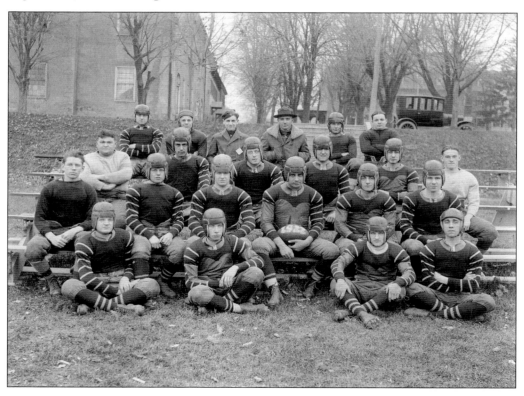

BASKETBALL. The image shows the 1923 basketball team. Basketball and baseball teams competed for the Hall against neighboring school teams.

BASEBALL. The Nazareth Hall baseball team is pictured here in 1915. The young men played baseball on their field across Center Street from the Hall.

CLASS PICTURES. This photograph shows the graduating class of 1914, posing in military uniform with guns and sabers.

FOURTH ROOM COMPANY. The youngest boys at the Hall were known as the Fourth Room Company and housed in the Schenck House on West Center Street.

Three

NAZARETH WELCOMES THE WORLD

Beginning in 1752 with the Rose Inn, and then the opening of the Nazareth Inn in 1771, Nazareth developed a reputation for hospitality. Nazareth became a convenient stopping point as roads were established for travel between Philadelphia and points north and New York City and points west. By 1914, the Nazareth area had 25 hotels operating and four trolley lines stopping in Nazareth to support travel and tourism.

Economic pressures and a changing country brought an end to the Moravian-only restricted community in 1856. The Borough of Nazareth officially became a municipality in 1858. This was a time of great change for Nazareth when an influx of youth came to work in the businesses that were now opening.

Industries including the Boulton Gun Factory and the C.F. Martin & Co., as well as textile and cement production provided employment opportunities. As a result, the population nearly tripled in three short decades from 949 in 1870 to an estimated population of 2,800 by 1904. Roads expanded in and around town, and trolleys were added to serve the expanding community.

New churches were built to serve the growing and diverse population, including Lutheran, United Church of Christ, and a Catholic church to serve the many Catholic people from various European countries who had immigrated to Nazareth.

Growth and expansion continued into the 20th century. Trolley service ended as the highway system developed, creating easy access to Philadelphia and New York City, and suburban development grew as a result. The school system merged to include Bushkill Township, Upper Nazareth, Lower Nazareth, Tatamy, and Stockertown. Today, Nazareth looks quite different, but the historic 18th-century buildings that remain contribute to Nazareth's distinctive character and identity.

THE NAZARETH INN. The reputation of the Nazareth Inn grew quickly after opening in 1771. Early on, two stagecoaches left the inn daily—one bound for Easton, the other for Bethlehem. The 20th century brought enlargement, additions, and modernization. By 1912, the inn had four stories with a bar, office, pool room, lobby, and a dining room located on the second floor. In 1968, the building was sold to Warren Dech, who established the Nazareth Hardware and Furniture store there.

THE AMERICAN HOTEL. The American Hotel was founded in 1853 by James W. Kemmerer, located at what was then the south end of Nazareth on Main Street. This photograph from about 1860 shows a large three-story brick building with a small balcony on the front.

THE BARONIAL HOTEL. The original part of this hotel was built in 1808, and in 1906 Clayton Heckman opened the hotel. Located at Main and Belvidere Streets across from the Nazareth Inn, the Baronial Hotel served as a hotel before being converted into the Leader Department Store in 1934. Along with the Inn, the Baronial was located at the end of one of the trolley lines in Nazareth, which promoted business. As a hotel, the large four-story redbrick building, with porches on two stories and a grand tower, offered a restaurant, bar, billiards, and "modern conveniences."

THE FRANKLIN HOUSE. The Franklin House was opened as a hotel by Aaron Fofel in 1860. A two-and-a-half-story redbrick building with gables in the front, the hotel became a popular place to watch horse and wagon traffic on South Main Street. It also served as a stagecoach stop, with a bar on the first floor and rooms on the second. In 1899, A.J. Stofflet purchased the building, turning it into a general store with his family's living quarters above. Currently, it houses Ralph's Appliance.

CHERRY HILL HOTEL. Built in 1862 north of the village of Schoeneck, the hotel had three stories with rooms for rent on the third floor. A fire destroyed the top of the building, and today there are only two stories. This c. 1898 photograph shows the original structure.

BOULTON GUN FACTORY. In 1798, fears of war with France led Pennsylvania's Governor Mifflin to place an order for 2,000 guns with William Henry II. When church authorities objected to Henry's request to build a two-story workshop and to employ outside labor in Nazareth, Henry built a new factory in Jacobsburg in 1798. That factory closed in 1803 when Henry completed his contract. A decade later, two of his sons, J. Joseph Henry and William Henry III, built this substantial gun factory, which they called Boulton.

HENRY FAMILY PICNIC. An elderly Granville Henry (1834–1912), with family and friends, enjoys a picnic in Henry's Woods. Henry's Woods, the Lehigh Valley's only remaining old-growth forest of deciduous trees and eastern hemlock, some of which are up to 130 feet high, has been preserved as part of the Jacobsburg Environmental Education Center, a 1,168-acre Pennsylvania state park. (Courtesy of the Jacobsburg Historical Society.)

THE HENRY FAMILY. The Henry family often went boating on the millpond formed by the dam that they built on the Bushkill Creek to power the Boulton gun factory. This boat, named the Lehieton (the Lenape name for the Bushkill Creek), survives in the collection of the Jacobsburg Historical Society. (Courtesy of the Jacobsburg Historical Society.)

HENRY FAMILY MEMBERS AT THE BOULTON GUN FACTORY. Henry family members pose in front of the Boulton gun factory, which was abandoned by the time that the Moravian minister D.C. Meinert took this photograph in 1908. Boulton was built between 1812 and 1813 by William Henry III (1794–1878) and his brother, J. Joseph Henry (1786–1836), who became the sole proprietor of Boulton in 1822. He was succeeded by his son James Henry and his grandson Granville Henry. Boulton produced rifles, pistols, and shotguns until 1895, providing substantial numbers of arms for Civil War soldiers and, thanks to the patronage of John Jacob Astor, for the western fur trade. Only traces of the foundation of the old gun factory remain today. (Courtesy of the Jacobsburg Historical Society.)

C.F. MARTIN AND COMPANY, INC. In 1839, Christian Friedrich Martin moved his home and business to Cherry Hill, just north of Nazareth. In August 1857, Christian Frederick Jr. bought the whole block on North Main Street from North Street to High Street, building his residence on the corner, with a workshop behind it, and in July 1859 the business moved to Nazareth. (Courtesy of the C.F. Martin & Co. Archives.)

C.F. MARTIN. This c. 1850 photograph is the earliest known image of Christian Friedrich Martin, who emigrated from Saxony to New York City in 1833. (Courtesy of the C.F. Martin & Co. Archives.)

NORTH STREET POLISHING. Martin acoustic guitars are prized for their tone, consistency, quality, and attention to handcrafted detail. Pictured here, Ken Smith Jr., started as a young man at North Street in the polishing area and transitioned to the repair department prior to his retirement in 1993. (Courtesy of the C.F. Martin & Co. Archives.)

NORTH STREET GUITAR PRODUCTION. The turn of the century brought the popularity of mandolins, banjos, and ukuleles, and necessitated three enlargements of the factory, in 1917, 1924, and 1925. By 1927, the craze for ukuleles had passed, and Martin returned to producing its most famous product, the Martin Guitar. (Courtesy of the C.F. Martin & Co. Archives.)

THE NAZARETH WAIST COMPANY. On May 24, 1886, the Nazareth Waist Company was organized on Belvidere Street by G.A. Schneebeli and Hans Jacob Nolde. Beginning with men's half-hose, the first stocking was knit on October 10, 1886, and the company prospered. In 1887, underwear, particularly women's shaped vests, was added to production. At this time, Nolde and Henry Kraemer, who had served as bookkeeper, left to open their own hosiery mill, the Kraemer Hosiery Company in Nazareth. Schneebeli continued alone, adding children's knit garments, underwear, stockings, and pajamas to the line. The Waist Mill, as it was known, prospered and was a pioneer in advertising its trademark—NAZARETH—throughout the United States and other countries. The workers of the Nazareth Waist Company are shown in the 1902 photograph below.

THE KRAEMER HOSIERY COMPANY. In 1887, when Henry Kraemer and Hans Jacob Nolde left the Nazareth Waist Company, they purchased what had been the Nazareth Foundry and, with 31 employees, began the Kraemer Hosiery Company. In 1888, Nolde returned to Reading, Pennsylvania, and Kraemer continued in business alone. Ladies' seamless stripes and lace hosiery were popular products. With new patents of innovative machinery, full-fashioned hose was introduced in 1899. On October 18, 1902, a fire destroyed all the facilities of the hosiery, but plants No. 1 and 2 were quickly rebuilt. A new dye house, a building addition, and 12 efficient machines imported from Germany gave Kraemer's world ranking. Building No. 5 was begun in 1921. (Below, courtesy of Kraemer Yarns.)

KRAEMER PRODUCTION LINE. By World War II, Kraemer's had become a leading producer of women's full-fashioned silk hosiery. But the war resulted in the unavailability of silk, and the advent of nylon and other changes in technology brought about the end of the hosiery business in Nazareth. In the 1950s, new spinning machinery was imported from Northern Ireland and installed. The original two carding machines and drawing and new spinning frames made the mill only one of four in the United States capable of spinning long staple synthetic fibers. Recognizing the changing nature of the business, on January 12, 1954, the business was renamed Kraemer Textiles, Inc., supplying the growing carpet business of that time. (Courtesy of Kraemer Yarns.)

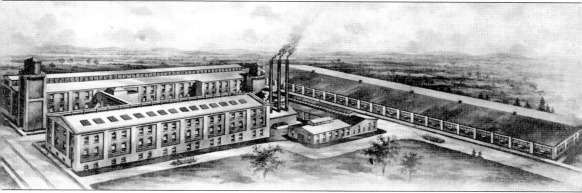

KRAEMER TEXTILE, INC. Arthur G. Schmidt, a former bookkeeper, succeeded Kraemer in 1907 and served until his death in 1934. His brothers Victor and Frank, along with Calvin H. Hartzell, succeeded him. In 2004, two Schmidt brothers, fourth-generation owners as textile manufacturers specializing in yarns for the apparel and home furnishing industries, saw hobbyists rediscovering knitting and craft and retail stores clamoring for yarn. Kraemer thus developed a line of colorful wool and acrylic-cotton blend yarns. Selling yarn and holding knitting and crocheting classes are presently a big part of the business, now called Kraemer Yarns. (Courtesy of Kraemer Yarns.)

THE UNANGST FOUNDRY AND MACHINE SHOP. In 1875, John J. Unangst completed the building for his new foundry, which produced farm implements. It was located on Belvidere Street between Whitfield and Cedar Streets. On July 24, 1879, a fire completely destroyed the plant. The photograph shows the cleanup effort underway.

THE NAZARETH BRICK COMPANY. As early as 1870–1875, Joseph Reich had a brickyard on Whitfield Street, while Charles Whitesell operated one on Main Street. In 1895, bricks were made by hand at a yard on Easton Road. These bricks had the name "Nazareth, PA" stamped into them. Succeeding these companies, Nazareth Face Brick Company was incorporated in 1934 to produce 15 million red bricks per year.

SCHOENECK FARMS. The alfalfa dehydration operation of Schoeneck Farms, Inc., began in 1931. As a division of Willow Dale Farms, a dairy operation, the dehydration plant used a tunnel-type, low-temperature drier. The plant, as well as the farm, used 4,000 acres to supply 5,000 tons of hay to process yearly. After the death of founder Arthur G. Schmidt, Robert A. Reichard purchased the business and continued the farming and dehydrating operations. Before the introduction of the mechanical forage harvester, about 50–60 men harvested, dried, and bagged the alfalfa meal.

SOUTH BROAD STREET. This idyllic view of South Broad Street in 1907 shows the original Union Church steeple in the background. The Union Church was built in 1859 to serve the joint Lutheran and Reformed congregations. The Union Church is the current location of the St. John's Lutheran Church.

KNECHT GROCERY. William Beitel established a general store at 68 South Main Street in 1810 and continued in business until 1865. Beitel was succeeded by his son John F. Beitel, who sold the business to Owen H. Knecht in 1876. The business was discontinued after Knecht's death in 1911.

THE H.F. ZIEGLER BUILDING. On the east side of South Main Street was the Ziegler building and residence. These are the original buildings of former Gustav H. Kern, whose business consisted of a boot and shoe store and a lumber yard.

JOHN E. SPEER, CIGAR MANUFACTURER. The Nazareth Directory of 1860 lists merchants of Nazareth. Among them are named Reuben Nolf, a "segar dealer," and John Hauan, a "tobacconist." By 1885, there were two cigar manufacturers listed in that year's directory. Pictured is John E. Speer's tobacco store on South Main Street. Speers is listed in an 1890 directory as a 38-year-old cigar maker with a wife, Emma, and five children.

NAZARETH VIGILANCE HOSE COMPANY. In 1839, Nazareth's first firehouse at the corner of Main and Chestnut Streets was used to house the fire equipment, including "the Good Intend," Nazareth's first fire engine. Years later, on May 10, 1897, a group of men met to organize Vigilance Hose Company, No. 1, a volunteer group that still exists. This group was a combination of two groups: the Moravian Fire Co., organized in 1791, and the Mechanic Fire Co., organized in 1812. In 1903, the firehouse on Belvidere Street, which is shown, was built. This was the town's firehouse and police station until 1980, when a new firehouse was built on South Broad Street.

THE NAZARETH ITEM PUBLISHING COMPANY. Dedicated to commercial printing and publishing a weekly newspaper called the *Nazareth Item*, this independent company's newspaper was devoted to literature, as well as local and general news. A favorite column about people and places in Nazareth was called "Dear Neighbor," written by a Nazareth resident, Sarah Brobst. Located on South Main Street, the *Nazareth Item* was published from 1891 to 1975.

C.E. KERN BUTCHER. In 1905, Clayton Kern opened a meat market on South Main Street. In 1908, Kern moved his business out of town, but continued serving Nazareth with butcher wagons and was recognized as the oldest active butcher in the community in 1940.

E.P. WAMBOLD HORSE SHOER. In 1896, Elmer P. Wambold began a blacksmith shop along Easton Road.

TRUMBOWER HOUSE. Pictured is the boyhood home of Nazareth businessman Peter S. Trumbower, on East Center Street.

THE TRUMBOWER COMPANY. On August 15, 1899, Peter S. Trumbower bought the former Charles Miksch coal yard along Tatamy Road. When, in 1902, the Lehigh & New England Railroad built a siding and coal pockets along Easton Road, Trumbower began a business there, which is pictured, including the sale of coal, lumber, crushed stone, and building materials. The company slogan was "Anything to Build Everything."

LEAVING FOR WAR. This photograph taken on the porch of the Baronial Hotel in May 1918 shows the enlisted men from the Nazareth area preparing to leave for World War I. Approximately 225 men left Nazareth to serve, with more than 100 serving overseas. Eleven sons of Nazareth gave their lives in this war.

NAZARETH NATIONAL BANK. In June 1897, Nazareth's first bank was built at 62 South Main Street. Nazareth National Bank expanded to 70–72 South Main in 1902. The services the bank offered grew along with its size, adding trust services in 1920. The bank's official name became Nazareth National Bank and Trust Company in 1929.

MAIN STREET, NAZARETH. This photograph, showing people gathering on both sides of South Main Street, was taken in the 1920s.

TROLLEYS. Passenger traffic was handled by electric railways, known as trolley lines. In 1899, the Bethlehem & Nazareth Passenger Railway Company was franchised to operate in Nazareth. In 1900, trolley connections were made with Easton via the Northampton Central Street Railway Company, and in 1901 a franchise was given to a line known as the Bangor-Nazareth Transit Company.

TROLLEY LINE. Trolleys ran along High, Main, Belvidere, and Mauch Chunk Streets. On Main Street, a trolley line ran east to Belvidere, New Jersey, while another ran west to Mauch Chunk (present-day Jim Thorpe), Pennsylvania, explaining the names given to Belvidere and Mauch Chunk Streets, which meet on South Main Street.

TROLLEY CRASH. This photograph shows the wreckage of the trolley crash that occurred on South Main Street in March 1920.

GAS STATION. The first gasoline station in Nazareth was located at the northeast corner of Main Street and Easton Road. The owner was J.H. Fulmer, who was also the Northampton County dealer for the Ford Motor Company. This photograph, taken in 1907, shows manager G. Frank Kratzer (left) and Matt Uhler.

GARAGE. This 1940 photograph shows the garage owned and operated by S.J. Gregory, which specialized in Studebaker sales and service. Gregory came to Nazareth from the Mack Truck Company in Allentown in 1915 and served as a mechanic for Harry Wunderly. That same year, Gregory took over the business as S.J. Gregory Auto Repair and Supply Shop.

THE NAZARETH CEMENT COMPANY. Soon after David Saylor discovered the cement properties of the Lehigh Valley, the Nazareth Cement Company built "the Old Mill" in 1898 and shipped cement early the next year as far west as Milwaukee and throughout the south. Organized as the first company in the Nazareth area by a group that included cement pioneers Wm. B. Schaffer and Conrad Miller, it began with seven small kilns, producing less than a thousand barrels per day. The company soon began a rapid expansion, changing ownership in 1901. Additional land was acquired in 1919 and again in 1926, when the mill had been almost completely rebuilt, completely electrified, and brought up to date.

PHŒNIX CEMENT MILL'S NAZARETH, PA.

THE PENN-DIXIE CEMENT CORPORATION. Shortly after helping to found the Nazareth Cement Company, William B. Schaffer disagreed with other directors and resigned, turning to promote in 1900 the Dexter-Portland Cement Company that began production the next year. In 1926, they merged with the Penn-Allen Cement Company in Bath as the Pennsylvania-Dixie Cement Corporation. They expanded, building 28 silos and increasing storage capacity to 300,000 barrels of cement. In 1928, the aerial tramway, over 10,000 feet long, carried crushed rock from the quarry at Plant No. 4 to Plant No. 5. This tramway of buckets crossed Route 248 between Nazareth and Bath and became a favorite sight to motorists. In 1971, the company was renamed Penn-Dixie Industries, Inc. In 1980, Penn-Dixie Industries declared bankruptcy and ceased all operations.

NAZARETH CEMENT. This aerial view of the Nazareth Cement Company, taken in 1935, shows the scale of operation at the time.

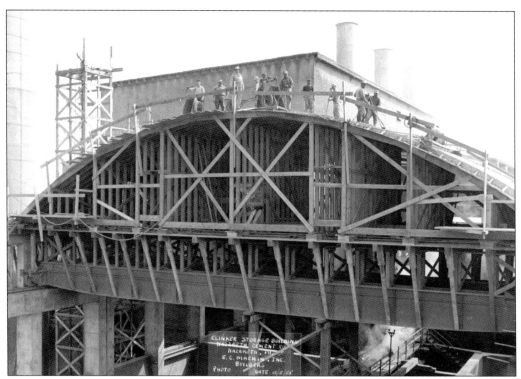

NAZARETH CEMENT OPERATIONS. In the 1950s, the company continued to modernize and improve production, as seen here with the construction of the new clinker storage building. (Courtesy of Lehigh Cement.)

NAZARETH CEMENT COMPANY QUARRY. The Portland cement industry for the United States was born in the Lehigh Valley. A narrow, but deep, band of limestone arcs just below the ground from eastern Berks County through upper Lehigh and Northampton Counties to western Warren County. The large cement plant on Route 248 in Nazareth is the heart of the company's operation. (Courtesy of Lehigh Cement.)

NAZARETH CEMENT COMPANY WORKERS, THE 1950s. The cement industry reached its pinnacle in 1956 by supplying the key material to create the interstate road system under Pres. Dwight D. Eisenhower's Federal-Aid Highway Act. Cement produced in Nazareth has been used in buildings and structures around the world. (Courtesy of Lehigh Cement.)

NAZARETH MORAVIAN CHURCH. In 1747, the Nazareth Moravian Congregation was incorporated. This church building, which continues today as the congregation's home, was built in 1861 as Nazareth's fourth place of worship. A separate parsonage was completed in 1875. The addition of a Sunday school wing and renovation of all three floors of the church began in 1958.

NAZARETH MORAVIAN CHURCH BELL. On August 31, 1840, the Nazareth church council decided to purchase a 600-pound brass bell in Philadelphia valued at $300. That bell was used by the 1840 Church and was later installed in the current church's belfry, as shown in this photograph.

St. John's Lutheran Church. The cornerstone of this church was laid on August 31, 1908, and it was dedicated on September 25, 1910. This church is located on the same site, the southwest corner of Broad and Prospects Streets, as the original St. John's Union Church that was dedicated on October 29 and 30, 1859. The union between Lutheran and Reformed congregations would last until 1905, when an agreement was made to dissolve the Union Church. The Lutheran congregation retained the building. A new Christian education building was dedicated on October 15, 1961, with many improvements occurring over the ensuing years. (Courtesy of St. John's Lutheran Church.)

St. John's United Church of Christ. In 1906, under Rev. Wallace H. Wotring, St. John's Reformed Church was built on the northeast corner of Broad and Prospect Streets, situated diagonally across from where they had worshipped as a Union church. Nazareth's St. John's United Church of Christ came into being on June 25, 1957, with the merger of the Congregational Christian Churches and the Evangelical and Reformed Church. Prior to that date, the church was known as St. John's Evangelical and Reformed Church. In 1957, a new Christian Education building was added. After 1966, a parsonage was built and St. John's Nursery School was begun.

SCHOENECK MORAVIAN CHURCH. On October 6, 1889, the congregation worshiped in a new church with a new organ. A new bell was added the next year, and after 1914, a brick addition was added to accommodate the Sunday school, and other rooms were added and remodeled. In 1958, a picnic pavilion was built on the church grounds, and a separate Christian education wing was added.

HOLY FAMILY ROMAN CATHOLIC CHURCH. On November 8, 1908, on West Center Street, the first mass was said at Holy Family Roman Catholic Church by Father Peter Fuengerlings. Within two years, a parochial school on the west side of Convent Avenue opened under the direction of the Sisters of the Most Sacred Heart of Jesus from the Convent at Reading. In 1911, the rectory was erected, and a convent was built in 1927. A new gymnasium opened in 1956, and Holy Family became active in promoting local sports programs. Ground was broken for a new church building in 1964 (pictured below), and it was dedicated on May 15, 1965. (Both, courtesy of Holy Family Parish.)

WHITFIELD SCHOOL STUDENTS. This photograph shows children lined up outside of the Whitfield School, on September 8, 1954, for the first day of school.

Whitfield School, Nazareth, Pa. 1916

13849

WHITFIELD SCHOOL. In 1884, the Whitfield School was built on East Chestnut Streets, behind the North Broad Building. Wings were added until the school contained 10 rooms.

NAZARETH HIGH SCHOOL, BROAD STREET BUILDING. In 1891, the first Nazareth High School was organized in the building now known as the North Broad Building. The first class of 57 students graduated in 1893. Grades 9 through 12 were schooled there until 1924, when the new high school on Belvidere Street was completed. Rooms in the North Broad Building later housed grades 5 and 6, and before closing, it held some district offices.

FAIRVIEW SCHOOL. The Fairview School was built in three stages in 1901, 1905, and 1921. Located at the corner of South Broad and Park Streets, it officially opened to students in 1902. The school was so named because it overlooked the Nazareth Fairgrounds, which occupied land between Broad and Main Streets and Park and South Streets. The school had eight rooms for grades one through six until 1963. The borough took possession of the building in 1969 and demolished it to create a playground.

NAZARETH HIGH SCHOOL, BELVIDERE STREET. In 1924, a new high school was built on Belvidere Street. It had 12 classrooms, an auditorium, gymnasium, locker and shower rooms, a health room, and a laboratory. The school was located on a tract of 13 acres, allowing for athletic fields, tennis courts, and play areas. An addition was built in 1930–1931. With a decision in 1952 to build the present senior high school on East Center Street, the school on Belvidere Street became the Nazareth Junior High School. The new senior high school graduated its first class in 1956.

HOLY FAMILY SCHOOL. In September 1910, the Sisters opened the doors of Holy Family School with 40 students on the second floor of the church on Center Street. The Sisters resided in quarters on the second floor adjacent to the classrooms until a convent was built in 1928. That second-floor school was replaced with the current school building on November 16, 1954.

GROUND BREAKING. The ceremonial brick is laid for the ground breaking of the new school in 1954. (Courtesy of Holy Family Parish.)

Nazareth High School Graduation. In 1940, honoring the town's bicentennial year, Nazareth High School held its graduation ceremony at the Nazareth Borough Park on June 27, beginning at 8:00 p.m. The above photograph shows a semicircle with Dr. George Wm. McClelland (handing out a certificate), Florence Nicholas, Wm. M. Bennett Jr., Mildred Moyer, Rae Beisel, Alice Beck, Betty Ackerman, and Henry W. Nickel.

Procession. The seniors' procession heads toward the park's amphitheater. This was the 44th commencement of Nazareth High School.

GRADUATION, 1940. A graduate shares her diploma with others on the stage. The class of 1940 leaves the amphitheater after their graduation ceremony at Nazareth Borough Park.

NAZARETH BAND. The Nazareth Band, also known as the Nazareth Brass Band, was organized in 1850. On August 16, 1858, the band provided the music for Nazareth's celebration of the laying of the transatlantic telegraph cable. In 1871, the band became known as the Nazareth Cornet Band. The band was incorporated in October 1895. After nine directors, the band's last meeting was on January 30, 1973.

NAZARETH BAND, PARADES. Marching in Nazareth parades, the Nazareth Band was very popular with local residents. The man in the derby is identified as the band's leader, John Reinheimer, in the late 1880s. The band is also shown standing in front of the Blue Ribbon Vehicle Store, an agricultural building at the Nazareth Fairgrounds.

NAZARETH BAND AT THE PLEASURE GARDENS. In 1935, the band members posed in the area of the Pleasure Gardens. The Pleasure Gardens were a favorite place for musical performances.

NAZARETH BAND AT THE WORLD'S FAIR. With Carl Seyfried conducting, the Nazareth Band played at the New York World's Fair on August 6, 1939.

NAZARETH MORAVIAN CHURCH TROMBONE CHOIR. From the earliest times in Moravian Church history, music, both vocal and instrumental, have been vital parts of Moravian worship and gatherings. On Easter, in the dark early morning hours, the Nazareth Moravian Brass Choir travels through the town, stopping to play chorales under street lights where members of the congregation live. They play to announce the joy of the risen Lord and to invite members to worship together at the sunrise service at God's Acre, overlooking the town.

WHITEFIELD HOUSE MUSEUM. In 1871, John Jordan Jr. purchased the Whitefield House and presented it to the Society for the Propagation of the Gospel as a home for retired or furloughed Moravian ministers and missionaries. He stipulated that the second floor be perpetually reserved for use by the Moravian Historical Society and its museum. This photograph of the original museum display on the second floor of the Whitefield House Museum shows the extensive collection of objects on display.

FIRST PUBLIC LIBRARY. On December 7, 1944, the third anniversary of the bombing of Pearl Harbor, citizens of Nazareth decided to erect a permanent memorial to Nazareth residents who had served their country. The first public library in Nazareth was named the Memorial Library of Nazareth and Vicinity on May 19, 1946. The library opened on Memorial Day 1951 on the land known as the Nazareth Hall Parade Field.

NAZARETH MEMORIAL LIBRARY. In May 1970, the contents of the library were moved into a new location, the previous home of Peter and Katherine Trumbower, whose heirs offered the home on East Center Street to the Borough of Nazareth. George Hahn, a Nazareth contractor, had built the stately brick home for the Trumbowers in 1927. This current library was the first historic building in Nazareth to receive a historical marker. (Courtesy of the Memorial Library of Nazareth and Vicinity.)

Sons of the Veterans & Auxiliary. On June 25, 1901, Capt. Owen Rice Camp No. 20, of the Sons of Veterans, was organized with 51 charter members. Twenty years later, on January 7, 1921, a Sons of Veterans Auxiliary was organized with 77 members. The Sons of Veterans had their own marching band and participated in community ceremonies and parades, including those celebrating the 1940 bicentennial.

Funeral Procession for Harold Van Horn Knecht. Private Knecht, a Nazareth native, was the first soldier from Pennsylvania killed in action during World War I. When Nazareth veterans, home from the war, formed a chapter of the American Legion in August 1920, there was no question that Post 415 would be called the Harold V. Knecht Post 415 of the American Legion.

POST OFFICE EMPLOYEES. Post office workers pose for this photograph in March 1911. The first post office in Nazareth was established on June 1, 1904.

THE POST OFFICE. Located just north of the Circle, the New Deal post office was built in 1936. One of its historic features is the mural *Cement Industry*, completed with Treasury Section of Fine Arts funds in 1938. The mural was painted by Ryah Ludins, one of the few female mural artists working with the WPA (Works Progress Administration). It can be seen in the Nazareth Post Office to this day.

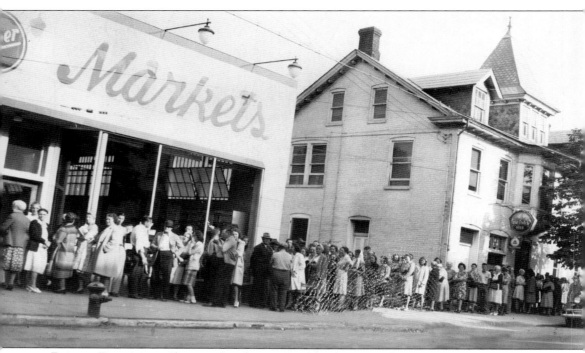

BUTTER RATIONING. Shoppers lined up to purchase butter at the ACME, American Store, on South Main Street. Rationing was part of life during World War II, and by the end of 1942 there was a serious shortage of butter and other fats. Points were assigned to each type of fat based on scarcity. Grocery stores posted the required ration points along with prices. Butter required a higher number of points than margarine.

UNANGST DEPARTMENT STORE. The Unangst Department Store was located at the southeast corner of East Belvidere and South Broad Streets. This general store was founded by John Jacob Unangst (1832–1897) in 1874. His son Edward J. Unangst joined the firm in 1883 and took over the management when John died. Edward's sons, in turn, became partners in the firm in 1917. It was then renamed E. J. Unangst & Sons, a name under which it continued doing business until closing in 1941. The building was later occupied by Nazareth Sporting Goods.

NAZARETH MOTEL. Located on Route 191 near the race track, the Nazareth Motel was packed with fans on Nazareth Speedway race weekends. Many clients returned, year after year, to stay at the motel. With 12 rooms, the motel also featured a restaurant and bar.

BICENTENNIAL CEREMONY. In 1940, Nazareth celebrated its 200th anniversary. At 4:00 p.m. on June 22, 1940, the community of Nazareth gathered at the Nazareth Borough Park amphitheater to officially begin the celebration. The event featured a religious service, music by the Nazareth Band, and an address by the governor of Pennsylvania, and it ended with an address by Judge William G. Barthold of Northampton County Courts.

BICENTENNIAL CELEBRATION AND PARADE. From June 22 to July 7, bicentennial activities included pageants, parades, costume balls, ringing bells and blowing whistles, three evenings of firework displays, a four-county firemen's convention, a track-and-field meet, Boy and Girl Scout events, a Children's Day, an Agricultural Day, a water carnival, a Military Day with a drum and bugle corps competition, a Pennsylvania Dutch play, archery and rod and gun competitions, band concerts, bicycle races, a soapbox derby, and many religious ceremonies. The town was decorated with flags on the streets, around Center Square, and on many homes and businesses. Andrew G. Kern served as general chairman of the bicentennial committee.

Boy Scouts. The official opening bicentennial parade began at 2:00 p.m. on June 22 with Boy Scouts and Sons of Veterans escorting Pennsylvania governor Arthur H. James. Boy Scout and Cub Scout troops have been active in Nazareth since the movement began at Nazareth Hall Military Academy in 1911. Maj. H.J.F. Reusswig, an instructor at the boys' school, organized Troop Veteran 1. In 1926, Troop 1 was received into the Easton Council of Boy Scouts as Troop No. 32, soon becoming the highest-rated troop in the council. This troop won many awards over the years, in sports, in efficiency, and in service, with several scouts earning the rank of Eagle Scout. The greatest achievement of this troop, however, was inspiring others in Nazareth and the vicinity to form new troops, including Troops 79, 44, 43, 42, 45, 78, and 79.

BICENTENNIAL PARADE BANDS. Marching bands, including those pictured from the neighboring towns of Wind Gap and Bangor, helped Nazareth celebrate its first 200 years.

PARADE PARTICIPANTS. On July 4, 1940, Nazareth held a Labor and Industry Parade as part of its 200th-year celebration. The Nazareth High School Marching Band leads the United Cement, Lime, and Gypsum Workers.

GARMENT WORKERS. Shown marching are garment workers from the Nazareth Waist Company, makers of underwear, sleepwear, and garments for all.

BICENTENNIAL MOMENTS. Part of the 1940 celebration involved a Nazareth Beauty Contest for young girls, who are shown here with the judges. Charming parade participants, such as the young couple in a horse-drawn cart pictured below, delighted the spectators in one of many parades.

BICENTENNIAL CELEBRATIONS. Band and drum and bugle corps competitions and marches of individual Nazareth organizations and groups were almost daily occurrences during the two-week celebration.

GIRL SCOUTS. Shown here in 1940, this group of Girl Scouts presented a drama, *Scouting in War-torn Countries*, for the bicentennial celebrations. In the spring of 1927, the Girl Scouts had organized in Nazareth as a troop of Tenderfoot Scouts. The troop first appeared in uniform as the Lone Troop in the Nazareth Memorial Day parade of 1928. Nazareth formed its own council in 1927 and organized its first Brownie Pack in September of that year. The Girl Scouting movement became so popular that, within a year, five scout troops and four brownie packs were added. Almost 20 troops in the Nazareth area have been active.

BICENTENNIAL COMMITTEE. Pictured at the Whitefield House are esteemed Nazareth residents who researched, wrote, and compiled the book *History of Nazareth Penna, 1740–1940: Two Centuries of Nazareth*, published by the committee in 1940.

NAZARETH FAIRGROUNDS. In November 1853, a committee of citizens of Nazareth bought eight acres of land at $80 per acre on which to hold the Northampton County Agricultural Fair. The fairgrounds extended from Main Street to Broad Street and from Park Street to the tracks of the Delaware, Lackawanna & Western Railroad (DL&W) below South Street. The first exhibition was held from September 26 to 28 in 1855. Gate receipts from those three days totaled $1,560. In 1899, the new site of the fairgrounds, the area of the present Giant grocery store, was purchased. In 1930, the exhibition space there was deemed no longer profitable and was closed.

NAZARETH FAIRGROUNDS AND RACETRACK. The Nazareth Fairgrounds, laid out in 1854, was used initially for sulky races (harness racing involving two-wheel carts). The fairgrounds contained a track, grandstand, and a performers' platform. The fairgrounds hosted the annual agricultural exhibition from 1855 to 1899. In 1930, the Nazareth Fairgrounds closed with two days of automobile racing. The grounds were sold in 1931.

NAZARETH YMCA. This photograph shows a swimming lesson taking place in the original swimming pool built in 1916. The YMCA, Young Men's Christian Association, has been a center for many residents since 1916. The previous "Y" building was expanded in 1989 to include a new pool area and locker rooms to replace the old indoor pool in the gym area of the Y. (Courtesy of the Greater Valley YMCA.)

BOWLING AT THE NAZARETH YMCA. Early on, the wooden bowling alleys in the Y, as it is called, were very popular to young and old alike. In 1982, the bowling alleys were converted to a weight training and fitness area. (Courtesy of the Greater Valley YMCA.)

111

NAZARETH BOROUGH PARK POOL. Constructed in 1937 as a WPA project, the 18,500-square-foot oval pool was the summer home for generations of Nazareth families. The 1937 pool was replaced in May 2015 with a state-of-the-art, 9,000-square-foot pool with water features, slides, competition lanes, and diving boards.

NAZARETH BOROUGH PARK. The popular swimming pool is a highlight of the park. The borough park also offers a baseball field, tennis courts, basketball courts, a log cabin, and pavilions for picnicking as well as playground equipment. Shown here is the original pool.

NAZARETH 250TH ANNIVERSARY PARADE. In 1990, Nazareth celebrated its 250th anniversary with activities spanning the months of May, June, and July. Events included a Miss Nazareth contest, a block party, bicycle race, a four-county firemen's parade, a concert by Tom Chapin, a talent show, and a service of thankfulness held in the amphitheater of the borough park. That event was preceded by three days called Heritage Ethnic Days, a custom and classic car show, an old-timers baseball game, walking tours, various pageants, shows, and contests. A gala anniversary banquet was held on June 29, 1990.

MARTIN GUITAR IN THE NAZARETH 250TH ANNIVERSARY PARADE. Employees of the C.F. Martin & Co. built a giant guitar float for the Nazareth 250th anniversary parade.

EDUCATORS. Educators from all schools in the Nazareth School District also participated in the parade with several education-inspired floats.

KIWANIS CLUB PARADE FLOAT. With 25 members, the Nazareth Kiwanis Club was chartered on February 22, 1972. They participated in the parade with this "Miss Nazareth" float. Other Nazareth service organizations also participated, including the Nazareth Lions Club, which has served Nazareth since its founding on June 5, 1924.

GRAND PARADE. Culminating the months of celebration, on Saturday, June 30, at 2:00 p.m., a grand parade was held along borough streets. Closing ceremonies were held that evening at 8:00 p.m. at the high school football field, Andrew S. Leh Stadium. On Saturday, September 15, a time capsule was buried at Nazareth Borough Hall to commemorate the anniversary year and Nazareth's 250 years.

HALLOWEEN PARADE. Nazareth children have been excited by the annual Halloween parade for decades. The event was originally held in the evening, and the darkness added to the spookiness of the costumed paraders and many floats. Today, the parade is held mid-October in the afternoon.

Four

PUTTING NAZARETH ON THE MAP

Today, Nazareth is perhaps best known as the hometown of auto-racing legend Mario Andretti and as the headquarters to the world-class Martin Guitar Company.

Mario Andretti was born in Montona, Italy, now Croatia, on February 28, 1940. In 1955, he and his family of five immigrated to America. Mario and his twin brother Aldo thought that their dream of becoming race car drivers was over. Settling in Nazareth, the family had just $125 and did not speak English. Imagine the thrill when Mario and Aldo discovered a race track right near their home. It was a half-mile dirt oval—different than what they had seen in Europe, and the cars were modified stock cars, not sophisticated Grand Prix cars. But there was a lot of speed. With some local friends, they modified a 1948 Hudson Hornet Sportsman, racing it for the first time in March 1959. While Aldo did not have the same good fortune due to injury, Mario's career flourished.

Mario Andretti went on to become one of the most successful American race car drivers in the history of the sport. He took the checkered flag 111 times during his career—a career that stretched five decades and across six continents.

The Martin Guitar Company, founded by Christian Frederick Martin Sr. in 1833, remains the oldest surviving maker of fine acoustic guitars in the world. For well over a century and a half, the company has continuously produced acoustic instruments in Nazareth that are acknowledged to be the finest in the world.

In 1986, C.F. Martin IV (the sixth-generation Martin to manage the company) became chairman of the board and chief executive officer. Under his leadership, the company has grown, and in 2004, it produced its millionth guitar. It now has a workforce of more than 600 employees. Martin is also one of the world's largest manufacturers of musical strings.

The list of Martin players, past and present, reads like a who's who of the musical world and includes legends such as Elvis Presley, Paul McCartney, Eric Clapton, Hank Williams Sr., Neil Young, Joan Baez, Paul Simon, Sting, Willie Nelson, and Johnny Cash.

NAZARETH RACETRACK. The original half-mile dirt racetrack for stock car racing, once the Nazareth Fairgrounds, was built in 1955. Many Sunday nights, residents of the town and Lower Nazareth Township, where the track was located, heard the rev of the dirt car engines and watched the dust cloud rise over the track as the cars raced. In 1969, the year that Mario Andretti won the Indy 500, he also won the race at this local track. In 1987, Roger Penske bought the uncompleted Nazareth National Speedway and paved the track. He renamed it the Pennsylvania International Raceway. The first event was held there in September of that year with Michael Andretti winning the CART race.

MARIO ANDRETTI. Mario Andretti brought fame to his hometown of Nazareth when he won the Indianapolis 500 on May 30, 1969. Here he is in the winner's circle, a wreath around his neck, with a bottle of cold milk—the traditional drink of Indy 500 winners! To honor this win, Nazareth renamed Market Street, where the Andrettis resided, to Victory Lane. (Courtesy of the Mario Andretti Archives.)

CELEBRATING AT THE DAYTONA 500. Mario Andretti and his wife, Dee Ann, celebrate Mario's first-place finish at the 1967 Daytona 500, NASCAR's biggest race. Some in the media viewed Mario's win over the regulars on the stock-car circuit with mixed emotion. One newspaper headline, in particular, stands out: "All of Dixie Mourns Andretti's Victory." Mario is the only driver to have won the prestigious trifecta: the 1967 Daytona 500, the 1969 Indianapolis 500, and the 1978 Formula One World Championship. (Courtesy of the Mario Andretti Archives.)

MARIO AND MICHAEL.
Though Mario
Andretti's career was
still very much in
gear, his son Michael's
career was really
taking off in 1983,
as symbolized by the
father tossing a helmet
to his son. Though
he did not surpass his
father's unparalleled
records, Michael
went on to amass 42
race victories and is
statistically one of
the most successful
drivers in the history
of American open-
wheel car racing.
(Courtesy of the Mario
Andretti Archives.)

FOUR GENERATIONS OF ANDRETTIS. This photograph was taken in April 1987. Pictured are Michael Andretti (left), Alvise Luigi "Gigi" Andretti (Mario's father), and Mario Andretti, holding Marco Andretti. Mario's roots remain in Nazareth, where he met his wife, Dee Ann, and raised three children, Michael, Jeff and Barbie, and where he still lives. Since Mario's retirement from competition, the racing tradition continues with Michael and Jeff, nephew John, and grandson Marco. (Courtesy of the Mario Andretti Archives.)

C.F. Martin & Co.'s New Factory. Most likely because of the huge backlog of orders, Frank Herbert Martin was able to convince his reticent and traditional father, C.F. Martin III, to build a modern factory. At the peak of the folk music boom in 1963, architects Fulmer and Bowers from Princeton, New Jersey, completed their vision for the new Sycamore Street Martin facility. After more than 100 years, the North Street Martin factory would cease to be the place where Martin guitars were made. (Courtesy of C.F. Martin & Co. Archives.)

C.F. Martin & Co. Production Line. The new factory provided better lighting and greater space—all on one level, as opposed to the many floors of North Street. This allowed for a much more efficient layout in what C.F. Martin III liked to call "an assembly line of hand-craftsmanship." Here, workers are fine shaping necks for Martin's very popular soprano ukuleles. (Courtesy of C.F. Martin & Co. Archives.)

C.F. MARTIN & CO. CELEBRATES NEW FACTORY. Tom Paxton made a name for himself in the early 1960s Greenwich Village folk scene with songs like "The Last Thing on My Mind." When the grand opening of the new factory was being planned in 1964, Frank Martin invited Tom to entertain from the loading platform of the new plant. (Courtesy of C.F. Martin & Co. Archives.)

JUDY COLLINS PERFORMS ON LOADING DOCK. Like Paxton, Judy Collins was basking in the folk limelight in 1964 with her third album that featured songs of her folk compatriots, including Bob Dylan and Pete Seeger. She joined Paxton in a performance from the loading platform. Appropriately, both Paxton and Collins returned to Martin on October 25, 2006, for the grand reopening of the new museum and visitor center. (Courtesy of C.F. Martin & Co. Archives.)

SIGNATURE EDITION MODELS. In 1995, Nazareth was well represented at the Royal Albert Hall in London for the presentation of Eric Clapton's 000-42EC signature edition. Martin established a line of signature editions that year, and the most successful of these limited edition models was the Eric Clapton model. His *MTV Unplugged* performance in 1992 spurred great interest in the Martin guitars he was playing, resulting in an unprecedented collaboration with Clapton that spanned two decades and created more than 10 popular signature editions. Pictured left to right are Dick Boak, Martin's director of artist relations; Martin CEO C.F. Martin IV; Eric Clapton; and Susan Ellis. (Courtesy of C.F. Martin & Co. Archives.)

About the Moravian Historical Society

Founded in 1857, the Moravian Historical Society is a not-for-profit organization that shares the history of our community and the fascinating contributions of the Moravians to worldwide culture, through public programs, guided tours, and engaging museum exhibits. The Whitefield House Museum welcomes visitors from around the world and provides outstanding educational opportunities for those interested in history, art, and music. We care for 20,000 objects, photographs, and documents, and these primary sources help connect students, scholars, and the public to the stories of our past. Many of the items on exhibit are one of a kind or extremely rare, including the 1776 Tannenberg organ that was played for George Washington, an early Martin guitar, and the first violin made in America.

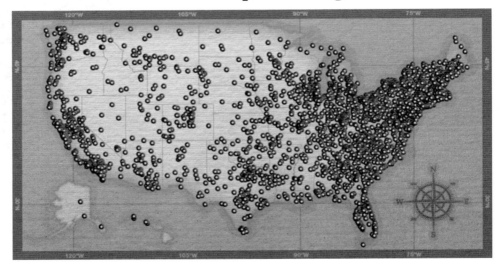